INDIAN AMERICA

A GEOGRAPHY OF NORTH AMERICAN INDIANS

by

MARIAN WALLACE NEY

illustrated by

LIBBY LAMBERT

PUBLISHED BY
CHEROKEE PUBLICATIONS
P.O. Box 124
CHEROKEE, N.C. 28719

TABLE OF CONTENTS

Introduction 3
Author's Preface 4, 5
Arizona 6, 7
California-Nevada 8, 9
Oregon-Washington. 10, 11
Canada-Alaska 12, 13
Montana 14, 15
North and South Dakota 16, 17
Wyoming-Idaho 18, 19
Utah-Colorado 20, 21
New Mexico 22, 23
Texas 24, 25
Mexico-Central America 26, 27
United States Map 28, 29
Missouri-Kansas-Nebraska 30, 31
Minnesota-Iowa 32, 33
Oklahoma 34, 35
Wisconsin-Michigan-Illinois-Indiana-Ohio 36, 37
Kentucky-Tennessee 38, 39
North Carolina 40, 41
Florida-Alabama-Georgia-South Carolina. 42, 43, 44, 45
Mississippi-Louisiana-Arkansas 46, 47
Virginia-West Virginia. 48, 49
New York. 50, 51
Pennsylvania-New Jersey-Delaware-Maryland 52, 53
Maine-New Hampshire-Vermont-Massachusetts-Connecticut and Rhode Island 54, 55
Suggested Readings 56

INTRODUCTION

This book attempts to give the reader a clear picture of Indian Geography, the location of the various tribes and confederacies at their most significant historical time and place. We should remember that the tribes were always on the move. The Blackfeet, for example, migrated from the East, especially after horses and firearms arrived. The first tribe to get guns in a given area could and did immediately drive others out, as the Chippewa, or Ojibway, did when they were armed by the French. They immediately cleared the Lake Superior region, forcing the Sioux, Sauk and Fox west and south. The Sioux ended up short years later in the Dakotas, and the Sauk and Fox in Illinois. In these often-bewildering migratory patterns, a single selection of place has had to be made, preferably the one where the culture came to fullest flower, or where its most famous incidents took place.

Because the material is compressed, the book does not pretend to be a definitive geography. For that, the student would have to consult not one but many full-length books. (A bibliography of such references is appended.) However, there are advantages in a short but comprehensive approach, especially one in which maps are given equal space with text: the general reader is not overwhelmed with exhaustive detail, but can get a picture of what tribes were where on the continent at a single reading, and can refer back easily to single sections. The format uses the place names of modern American states to make that convenient.

In describing a tribe, there is emphasis on those individuals and events which best illustrate its special qualities. Perhaps most important, there is an attempt to deal with the very idea of geography from the Indian point of view; that is, not as an isolated subject, but one bound up with everything else — people, events, the past . . . everything.

A few details should be noted: Indian names did not and do not necessarily refer to the bearer directly. For example, Sitting Bull was not so named because he seemed to resemble a sitting bull (the usual interpretation), but because in his boyhood he had killed a sitting buffalo bull. Because an Indian was called Running Fox did not necessarily mean he ran like a fox; it is more likely that a running fox had played some part in his life.

PREFACE

Perhaps we make a mistake in trying to see the American Indian culture as a reality when it has actually become a myth, as far from us now as that of the Periclean Greeks. They were mythical from the beginning, misnamed by explorers who dreamed of India and Cathay and, in that dream, never really accepted the peoples on the North American continent as flesh and blood.

The immense pressure of European immigrants was not to be denied; it was obvious from the start that a whole continent could not be left to less than a million hunters as their private preserve. It was only a question of how it would be done. That it turned out as it did only served, again, to demonstrate the respective dreams. The Europeans brought their myth and sought to impose it on a land and a people. The Indians fought back to maintain their myth. The Europeans-become-Americans enjoyed the technical triumph; the Indians, we begin to see, won the spiritual battle.

There is even a parallel in Christianity itself, the early martyrs decimated by the Roman power, but gradually capturing the imagination of their conquerors. It doesn't matter any more that the Indians lost the formal battle; as the years go by we begin to wonder if they didn't win on another, deeper level. They were a religious people, and died for their beliefs; the modern American whites, shorn of all belief, wonder uncomfortably if it was not perhaps better to have gone that way than to linger on in the technological wasteland.

After a hundred years of vilifying Indians, the pendulum now swings the other way and there is danger of sentimental distortion in that direction. Indians were not perfect. However, they remain infinitely more sinned against than sinning. As General W. S. Harney, who fought the Teton Sioux, said: "I have lived on this frontier fifty years and I have never yet known an instance in which war broke out with these tribes, that the tribes were not in the right." No trapper, no mountain man, no soldier who knew the Indians (and who was not unbalanced, like Custer, for example) ever felt differently.

Returning to the Indians as myth, we begin to sense, perhaps, that they are the true American story. As Vine Deloria, the Sioux essayist, points out, the modern world finds it has much to learn from them. For instance, the Indian was an instinctive environmentalist, even during the most highly complex and developed cultures, as in Central and South America, living in harmony with nature as part of his faith. That attitude seemed meaningless or irrelevant to the early whites; it looms as a matter of life or death to whites today. Such learning is not, it should be pointed out, pious and superficial, but based on respect for superior insight.

Like all mythological peoples, the Indians as they were are gone forever. As gone for modern Indians as for modern whites. In the **American Heritage Book of Indians,** William Brandon wrote: "The wars of the plains are America's **Iliad** . . . all poetry, for poetry is really made of blood and not of daffodils. It will outlive sober history and never quite die . . . Red Cloud and Roman Nose will, very likely, still touch a light to the spirit as long as America is remembered." Meant that way or not, there is the implication that Red Cloud and Roman Nose will be remembered when all else American is forgotten. Indeed, the legend is already a world as well as a regional myth.

The invading whites, with their overwhelming superiority, were as strange and terrifying to the Indians as men from outer space armed with irresistible weapons would be to modern whites. Would whites go down as bravely, believing in their own gods to the end, singing the Death Song with the superb serenity of White Antelope, the Cheyenne war chief? That is the real yardstick, the test the Indians passed, their passport to mythology.

In **Out of Africa,** Isak Dineson wrote of her departure from that land, "It was not I who was going away, I did not have it in my power to leave Africa, but it was the country that was slowly and gravely withdrawing from me, like the sea in ebb-tide." The old Indian world has withdrawn from us in somewhat the same way, slowly and gravely, taking with it the essence of the land. If we ever want that essence back, we will have to come to peace with that world, with those departed immortals.

We understand this dimly, but with increasing perception. Tecumseh, Osceola, Joseph, Plenty Coups, Red Cloud, and all the others are our leaders as well. We may not know that consciously yet, but we reveal an unconscious understanding in inadvertant ways. As one example, the United States Army paratroopers of World War II, when jumping into combat, did not call on formal gods, country, wives or sweethearts, mothers or fathers. The word they cried out as they leaped from their planes, their last word for all they knew, given into the wind as both defiance of the enemy and prayer for life, was "Geronimo!" The Indian as myth-god-protector could not ask for deeper recognition, greater respect.

Marian Wallace Ney
Cherokee, North Carolina
April, 1976

Southern Paiute

Glen Canyon Dam

Navajo

Grand Canyon
Nat'l Pk.

*Lake
Mead*

**Hopi
Navajo**

*Hoover
Dam*

Havasupai

Little Colorado R.

Petrified Forest
Nat'l Pk.

Walapai

Mohave

Arizona

Tonto

Zuni

Colorado R.

Yavapai

Apache

Yuma

Gila River

Salt River

Hohokam

Organ Pipe
Cactus Nat'l Pk.

Gila River

Chiricahua

Saguaro
Nat'l Pk.

Pima

ARIZONA

The intimate position of geography in the lives and religion of the Indians probably is revealed more clearly in Arizona than in any other area. The variety of natural land forms is great, and so were the different tribal characteristics, as well as means of existence.

In the northeast is the home of the Navajo, a proud and independent people, today the largest of all the remaining tribes. The Navajo adapt to modern life only so far as they choose, and continue somewhat nomadic. In the center of Navajo country live the Hopi, a peaceable Pueblo people who keep to their terraced villages and adhere to old ways and to their own religion, which permeates their daily life down to the last detail, as it has for some 1500 years. In Canyon de Chelly, farms are still tended as they have been for 900 years. The Havasupai live along the Colorado River in the Grand Canyon. In the northwest corner of Arizona is the ancient home of the Walapai and the Yavapai.

The Hohokam, more developed than earlier Cochise Men, lived along the Gila Valley and built canals to irrigate their desert lands. The Yuma, Mohave, and Cocopa were all tribes closely attuned to and dependent upon the south-flowing Colorado River as it leaves the Grand Canyon. The Maricopa were forced out of their original lands by the Yuma, and joined the Pima and Papago to the east.

The Apache, definitive in terms of ferocity, are linked to the Navajo by language, as they are an Athabascan-speaking people. They did not have the strong central government of most other Indian cultures, being a scattered and nomadic people. As with the Hopi, family descent was in the line of the mother. All the Apaches were war-like, roving, and non-tribal, but the Mescalero and the Chiricahua Apaches were the outstanding fighters. To the Chiricahua belonged the famous Cochise, Nana, Geronimo, and Mangas Coloradas.

Arizona seems still very much the home of the Indian; the Great Spirit remains. National policy has always restricted the native American to non-productive land, but in Arizona some of that land is of unique and powerful beauty. Monument Valley and Canyon de Chelly are too overpowering for men of weaker religious bent. Even where the Indians no longer live, the landscape speaks strongly of them.

Karok

Shasta

Northern Paiute

Yurok

Pyramid
Lake

Humbolt River

Hupa

Gosute

Carson Sink

Yuki

Shoshone

Sacramento R.

Lake
Tahoe

Nevada

Wappo

Mono

Paiute

Yosemite
Nat'l Pk.

Washo

Panaca

Death Valley
Nat'l Pk.

Lake
Mead

Esselen

Sequoyah
Nat'l Pk.

LAS VEGAS

Paiute

Hoover
Dam

Yokuts

California

Serrano

Mojave

LOS
ANGELES

Joshua Tree Pk.

Colorado R.

Cumash

SAN
DIEGO

Salton
Sea

8

CALIFORNIA AND NEVADA

In the temperate climate of California once lived happy people known to history as the Mission Indians. According to John Collier, ". . . people only to be described through the language of music . . . joyously hospitable . . . free as birds, whose speech and colors were like the warbling and plumage of birds . . . Childlike they were, these natives, completely efficient toward their practical ends, within their wandering dance and song. For how many years had this man-nature garden of all bright colors grown? More than ten thousand years."

In a very short time the Spaniards despoiled this garden, and imprisoned the graceful inhabitants like beasts within mission walls, hence the ironic name Mission Indians. The area most densely populated by the natives in what was to become the United States was sacked and depopulated by murder, disease, and unendurable slavery. Food had been abundant and varied, and near-timeless and languid life had not prepared the natives to make the least sign of resistance to the ways of invading men; these innocent beings drifted voluntarily into the slavery which brought their end. The devastation of this garden was so complete that only the tiniest fragments of the past were left here and there.

Originally, there were many small groups scattered throughout this geographical region, including the Cumash, a larger band within the Hokan-speaking family. To the east, in the area of the Great Basin in what is now modern Nevada, were Indians of a brisker, more warlike mentality — the Shoshone and the Paiute. In the desert wastes lived a despondent and primitive group known as Digger Indians. The Washo lived in the region of Lake Tahoe, and the Yuma roamed where they chose.

It was the Paiute, Wovoka, of Nevada, who emerged from a prolonged trance with a vision depicting the Ghost Dance in the last period of Indian resistance, when most of the great tribes had already been shut up on the reservations along with their remaining leaders. The vision prophesied Indian survival on a continent swept clean of whites. It required the tribes to meet at certain times and dance out a specific religious symbolism so that the prophecy would be fulfilled. The government felt threatened by wide-spread dancing for such a purpose and moved to eliminate it, a decision which resulted in the ruthless slaughter at Wounded Knee.

CANADA

Colville

Columbia River

Wenatchee

Spokan

Washington

Palouse

Makah

Quinault

SEATTLE

Yakima

Snake River

Chinook

Wasco

Nez Perce

Clatsop

Klickitat

Cayuse

PORTLAND

Umatilla

HELLS CANYON

Columbia River

Kalapoola

Walla
Walla

Oregon

Siuslaw

Malheur
Lake

Klamath

Modoc

Shoshoni

CALIFORNIA

OREGON AND WASHINGTON

Along this coast was the home of the wealthiest Indians north of Mexico. In this context, wealth meant food, especially salmon. In the summer, these Pacific tribes could catch and dry enough food to last for a year. There were also cod, halibut, smelts, shellfish, sea otter, sea lion, and even whale. These peoples built large houses and sea-going canoes, carved the famous totem poles, and gave feasts known as potlatches.

From what is now the Oregon-California border to about the present American-Canadian border were what may be called the Inland Tribes, living on rivers and bays rather than on the ocean itself. They did not go whaling, their woodwork was mainly unpainted, and they were not noted for masks, feast dishes, or totem poles. The tribes included the Klamath, Modoc, Makah, Quinault, Chinook, Kalapoola, and Suislaw. Further inland in Washington and Oregon were such peoples as the Colville, Spokan, Palouse, Walla Walla, Cayuse, and Yakima, living much like their neighbors in Idaho, Montana, and other plateau states.

Related to these tribes, but living along the Canadian coast (see map of Canada and Alaska) into what is known as the panhandle of Alaska were the true Maritime tribes, the Nootka, Haida, Bella Coola, Kwakiutl, and Tlingit. These were the really rich, the sea-raiders, whalers, totem-builders and party-givers. The totem poles were not mentioned by visiting sailors until 1791, although ships had been touching along the coast for many years. We know that all the poles we now see were carved with iron tools (indeed, they could not have been executed without them) which were brought in by the sailors, and that many Chinese and Hawaiians in those crews remained to live with the Indians.

The white pioneers who first saw the enormous Indian houses on Puget Sound, as large as New England barns, could not believe they were made by Indians without using nails or saws to shape the huge trees, which were floated downstream to the sites.

The word "potlatch" comes from the Nootka **patshatl,** meaning "giving". The potlatches were feasts to celebrate any sort of occasion. Some of them took years to prepare for, and extravagant gifts were distributed: blankets, cedar chests, sea otter furs. They were actually squandering contests in which rival chiefs competed to see who could outdo the other. In the end, a chief would often kill a valuable slave with a special club and toss the scalp contemptuously to his rival, or destroy his invaluable copper plates, acts which have been compared to the white gesture of lighting a cigar with a $1000 bill.

11

Slave

Cree

Kaska

Beaver

Reindeer Lake

Lake Athabasca

Salish

Hare

Inuit

Bear Lake

Great Bear Lake

Great Slave Lake

Canada

Sekani

Bella Coola

Nootka

Kwakiutl

Haida

Tagish

Han

Athabascan

Kutchin

Mackenzie River

Tlingit

Tanana

Chuga

Chigmiut

Inuit

Koyukon

Brooks Range

Colville River

Alaska

Mt. McKinley Nat'l Pk.

Ingalik

Lliamma Lake

Katmai Nat'l Mon.

Malemiut

Yukon River

Aleut

12

CANADA AND ALASKA

Canada and Alaska would, of course, merit a complete study of their own. Limited information is included here to make our overview of North America complete.

Relations between whites and Indians in Canada were far less violent than in the United States. The early French put very little pressure on the tribes, and did not have the ingrained American feeling of racial superiority. Many of the French married Indians, and their children were taken into the white culture. The British were more stiffnecked, but also more realistic than the Americans in that they did not make treaties only to break them. They treated the Indians as subject peoples from the beginning, obliged to take what was given them. Surprisingly enough, this policy, harsh but honest, was relatively successful, and the Indians received more than might have been expected. White-Indian conflicts over land were practically unknown in Canada. Such clashes as did occur were a result of fur trade rivalries, or the French-English struggle. Reserves were granted from the beginning, and there was always enough land in Canada for both Indians and Whites.

The American-Canadian border was, of course, an unreal boundary line from the Indian standpoint, and most of the tribes along the northern part of what is now the United States were also in Canada.

Indians in Canada and Alaska fall into two large language groups: Algonkian and Athabascan. There is a third group, the Eskimo-Aleut, but Eskimos are not regarded as Indians, a point which should be kept in mind. Also, the language groups and tribes on the Pacific Coast are not mentioned here because they are covered in OREGON and WASHINGTON.

Unlike Indians in the United States, the Alaska tribes were not pushed off their lands, but kept the necessary land base for survival. In 1971, the United States passed the Alaska Native Claims Settlement Act, the largest land settlement to native Americans in its history. Under the terms of the Act, about one-twelfth of Alaska was turned over to the Alaska Native Corporations, especially formed groups, in a unique solution to Indian land claims. These regional corporations issue stock, invest money and conduct financial affairs for the people in the area. A total of forty million acres of land were turned over, plus a $500,000,000 federal appropriation and an equal sum in mineral royalties.

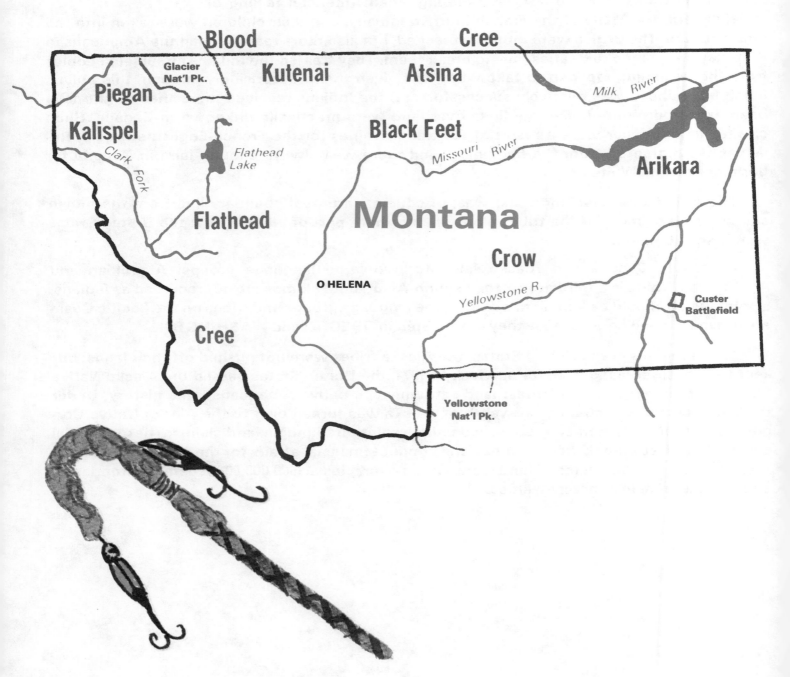

Blood

Cree

Glacier
Nat'l Pk.

Kutenai

Atsina

Milk River

Piegan

Kalispel

Black Feet

Clark

Flathead
Lake

Missouri River

Arikara

Fork

Flathead

Montana

Crow

O HELENA

Yellowstone R.

Custer
Battlefield

Cree

Yellowstone
Nat'l Pk.

MONTANA

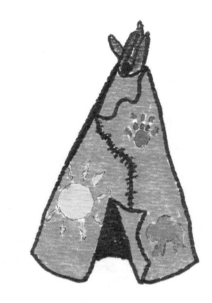

Another state steeped in Indian history, Montana was the home of such famous tribes as the Blackfeet, Cree, Crow, and Flathead. There were also Atsina, Arikara, Kalispel and Kutenai in Montana.

The Blackfeet Confederacy was the most powerful Algonkian-speaking group on the northern plains. They were divided into three independent tribes: the Blackfeet proper, or Siksika; The Piegan, or Pikuni (the name means poorly dressed); and the Kainah, or Blood Indians. (The term "Blood" probably comes from their habit of painting their bodies with red clay for certain ceremonies.) The Confederacy also included the Gros Ventre, or Atsina; and the Sarsi.

The Blackfeet were mighty warriors. They fought all their Indian neighbors, especially the Crow, and waged incessant war against the early fur trappers and traders, whom they suspected of being allies of the Crow. They were a handsome people, noted for their skill in the crafts, beautiful tipis, "straight up" bonnets, and their own form of the Sun Dance, which was centered around a woman. Their reservation in Montana, adjacent to Glacier National Park, is one of the most attractive in the United States.

The Crow were considered the most handsome of the western Indians, and perhaps the most handsome in North America. The men were noted for their long hair. Catlin, famed for his studies of Indian peoples, painted and described warriors on whom it not only reached to the ground but trailed behind. And required the whole morning to put up! If anything, it enhanced their ability as fighters. A relatively small tribe, they were able to hold their own against the formidable Blackfeet. The life of their last chief, Plenty Coups, spanned an amazing career. A scout for the Army at the time of the Custer massacre, he later became a farmer, and lived to act as the Indian chosen to represent all Indians at the dedication ceremony at the tomb of the Unknown Soldier in Washington in 1921. He closed the program by placing his war bonnet and coup stick on the grave. He was last because there was nothing to equal such a gesture. The Crow abolished the title of chief when Plenty Coups died because they felt there could never be another person worthy to follow him.

The Little Big Horn runs through the Crow Reservation in southeastern Montana, and there is the monument to the most famous of all Indian victories, the most famous and the last. It is not possible to walk that ground with indifference. Nor is it possible to give a single meaning or interpretation, for any person to feel just what another does. Under the soft Montana sky, one only knows it is forever a place where something of profound significance happened.

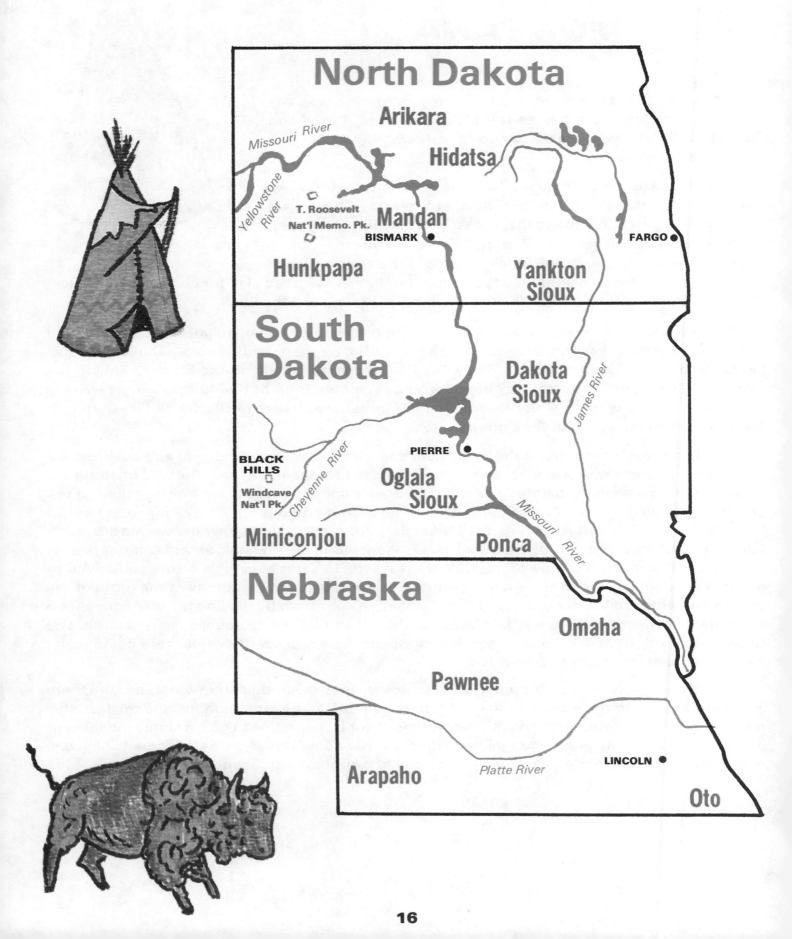

North Dakota

Arikara

Hidatsa

Missouri River

Yellowstone River

T. Roosevelt
Nat'l Memo. Pk.

Mandan

BISMARK ●

FARGO ●

Hunkpapa

Yankton
Sioux

**South
Dakota**

Dakota
Sioux

James River

PIERRE ●

BLACK
HILLS

Cheyenne River

Windcave
Nat'l Pk.

Oglala
Sioux

Missouri River

Miniconjou

Ponca

Nebraska

Omaha

Pawnee

Arapaho

Platte River

LINCOLN ●

Oto

NORTH AND SOUTH DAKOTA

From the Dakotas has come the most powerful example of Indian thought and life. The world first heard of the area through Lewis and Clark, who met with the Arikara and wrote memorable descriptions of Mandan villages and individual Indians. Many tribes have surged back and forth across the poetic landscape, but it is the Sioux who totally identified themselves with the earth here and its mysteries, and who, in turn, gave us the understanding of what such identification meant.

They were not indigenous to the area, but driven there by the Ojibways, or Chippewas, who were the first to receive guns from the French when the latter arrived in the Great Lakes area. Even the formidable Sioux were not able to face weapons so superior to their own bows and arrows, and they moved onto the Plains.

At first these Lakota (or Dakota) tribes carried on their nomadic hunting with dog travois, but with the advent of the horse in this area, their small but clearly defined civilization flowered. The horse travois made possible the larger, decorated tipis wherein the women created clothing with religious symbols stitched in. The self-discipline imposed by the rigors of wild life, the sense of community, and the instinctive desire to live with nature combined to bring forth an even stronger religious and moral sense. The Sioux had an elaborate and sophisticated code of behavior, understood by all.

With the possible exception of Tecumseh, a Shawnee, the Sioux chiefs made the most adamant resistance to the white man and his ways. These chiefs were articulate in their objections to his physical appearance, his religions, and his morality. They also objected to his inconsistency within his own system.

Such great Sioux chiefs as Red Cloud, Sitting Bull and Crazy Horse were not savages blindly resisting white "civilization" because they did not understand it and felt inferior to it. They were religious-political-military leaders, who understood it very well and found it inferior to their own very valid and operative civilization. They lost, but that did not shake their conviction that their civilization was superior to that of their conquerors.

The Sioux, particularly the Oglala Sioux, have since contributed many philosophers and writers, including Black Elk, Charles Eastman, and Vine Deloria, all dedicated to keeping alive that unique life, religion, and civilization.

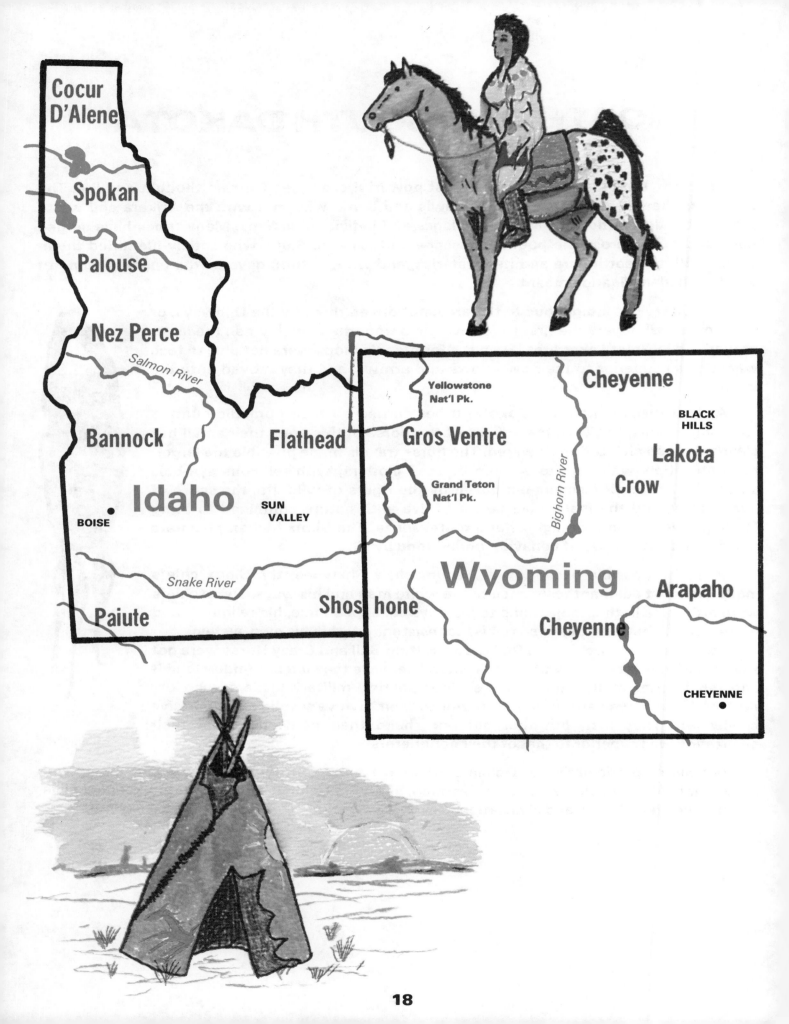

Cocur D'Alene

Spokan

Palouse

Nez Perce

Salmon River

Bannock

Flathead

Idaho

SUN VALLEY

BOISE

Snake River

Paiute

Shoshone

Yellowstone Nat'l Pk.

Gros Ventre

Grand Teton Nat'l Pk.

Cheyenne

BLACK HILLS

Lakota

Crow

Bighorn River

Wyoming

Arapaho

Cheyenne

CHEYENNE

18

WYOMING AND IDAHO

The famous Shoshone woman, Sacajawea, without whose help the Lewis and Clark expedition probably would not have succeeded, was born in Idaho. Other tribes in the Wyoming-Idaho area included the Spokan, Paiute, Palouse, Bannock, Coeur d'Alene, and Nez Perce. The last-named tribe lived in Idaho, and also in a part of Washington and Oregon. The Wallowa Valley, which the Nez Perce called the ''valley of the winding waters,'' had been theirs for centuries. When it was taken from them as Oregon opened up, Chief Joseph and those Nez Perce who lived in the valley decided to fight.

Joseph had not been a warrior, but he emerged as one of the greatest, and one of the world's true military geniuses. Rather than move onto a reservation, he decided to make for Canada. Pursued by white troops for 1800 miles through Idaho and Montana in the late summer of 1877, he brought his little band, the majority of which were women and children, sick, wounded and dying, to within fifty miles of the Canadian border. There he was forced to surrender unconditionally. He had outwitted the armies tracking him for months, and the trek is still studied by military tacticians. His last words on surrendering are probably the most quoted and best known of any ever spoken by an Indian: ''From where the sun now stands, I will fight no more forever.''

The history of the Cheyenne repeats the usual course of Indian-white relations, with special variations. In 1864, while camped at a place called Sand Creek on a peace mission, they were attacked by a Colonel Chivington at the head of a volunteer force of about a thousand. Chivington's battle orders were: ''Kill and scalp all, big and little.''

Black Kettle, a Cheyenne chief, ran up the white flag to no avail. He eventually escaped, but the Cheyenne war chief, White Antelope, refused to run and sang his death song with folded arms. The refrain, which has never been forgotten, went, ''Nothing lives long, except the earth and the mountains.'' About 200 Cheyenne women and children and 70 men were killed.

Many whites were disgusted with what was probably the greatest white victory on the plains in terms of Indians killed: Kit Carson referred to the white soldiers as cowards and dogs.

As a result, the frontier went up in flames, and the Cheyenne were in the forefront, led by Little Wolf and the legendary Roman Nose. Black Kettle, who wanted peace, was killed in the second deadly surprise attack by white troops, this one on the banks of the Washita River, along with over a hundred men, women and children. The commander on this raid was George Custer, whom the Cheyenne met for the last time, inevitably, with the Sioux at the Little Big Horn.

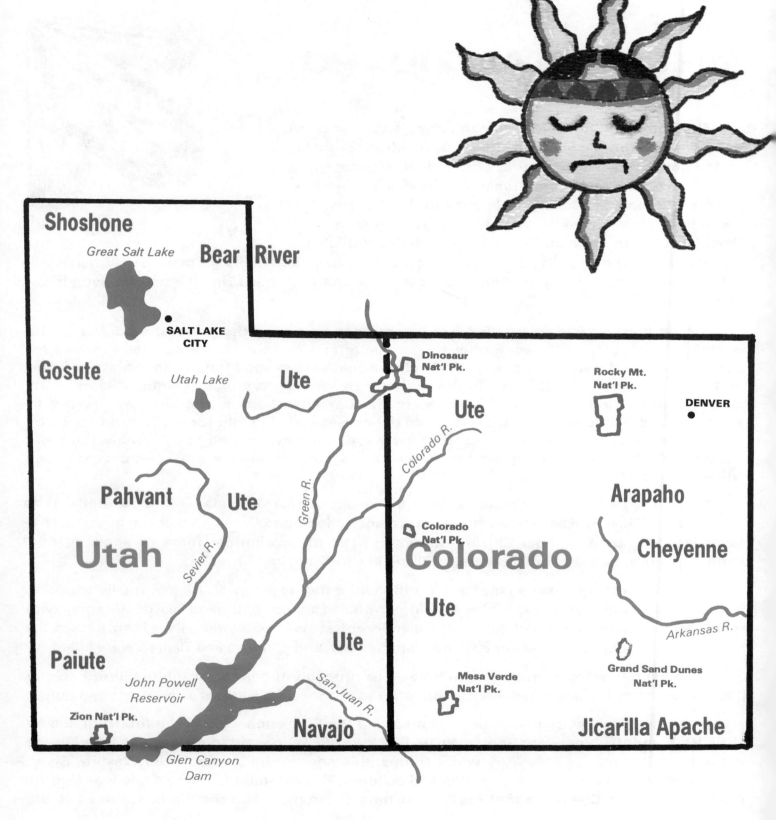

Shoshone

Great Salt Lake

Bear River

SALT LAKE CITY

Gosute

Utah Lake

Ute

Dinosaur Nat'l Pk.

Rocky Mt. Nat'l Pk.

DENVER

Ute

Pahvant

Ute

Green R.

Colorado R.

Arapaho

Colorado Nat'l Pk.

Utah

Sevier R.

Colorado

Cheyenne

Ute

Paiute

Ute

Arkansas R.

John Powell Reservoir

San Juan R.

Mesa Verde Nat'l Pk.

Grand Sand Dunes Nat'l Pk.

Zion Nat'l Pk.

Navajo

Jicarilla Apache

Glen Canyon Dam

UTAH AND COLORADO

In this region was part of the Great Basin area, one of the driest and most inhospitable places in the United States. And the Indians who lived in it were among the poorest in North America. They were remarkably ingenious in adjusting to such a hostile environment and finding food: grasshoppers were driven into trenches where they were roasted alive and then ground into flour; rats and lizards were jerked from their hiding places with wooden crooks, then killed; rabbits and birds were driven into tall nets.

Even when horses came, people such as the Paiute, in southwestern Utah, could not use them because there was no pasture. This tribe was often raided by the Apache and Navajo because they could not resist when armed horsemen kidnapped their children and sold them to the Spaniards.

Those just out of the grimmest part of the Basin, like the Utes, were able to use horses, and immediately became as warlike as any of the plains Indians. There were also some Commanche and Navajo in the Utah-Colorado area, and a sizable contingent of Arapaho.

The Arapaho had migrated from the western shore of Lake Superior. Their name comes from the Pawnee word **tirapihu** meaning "he buys, or trades," one of the primary activities of this tribe. They were linked with the Cheyenne in raids on the Mexican settlements in the Southwest. They also fought the Shoshone, Ute, Navajo and Pawnee, and some were with the Sioux at the Little Big Horn.

They made peace with the United States in 1861, at Fort Wise, Kansas, and signed the Medicine Lodge Treaty in 1867. They were then split into the Northern and Southern Arapaho. The Northern were put on a reservation at Wind River, Wyoming, which they share with their old enemies, the Shoshone. The Southern were shipped to Oklahoma, where they live with their traditional allies, the Cheyenne. Known as a deeply religious people, they still perform their Sun dance in a circular medicine lodge on the Wind River Reservation, an impressive ceremony which draws Indians from many other tribes.

San Juan River

TAOS (BLUE LAKE) ●

Canadian River

Tiwa

Conchos Reservoir

SANTA FE ●

Tano

● ALBUQUERQUE

Jicarilla

Rio Grande River

Tewa

Keres

Tano

Acoma

Pecos River

Piro

Zuni

New Mexico

Chiricahua Apache

White Sands Nat'l Mon.

Mogollon

Carlsbad Caverns Nat'l Pk.

Manso

Mescalero

NEW MEXICO

Like Arizona, New Mexico is primarily the land of the pueblo-dwelling peoples. It speaks strongly even today of Indian life and thought continuing from a remote past. The Anasazi-speaking people of Acoma occupied their mesa city for over 600 years, and once there were seventy pueblos in the area bounded by the Pecos, Taos, and the Grand Canyon. The Zuni speak a language unrelated to any other in the Indian world; the Hopi a Shoshone dialect; and the others speak Tano or Keres dialects. The pueblos are ruled by councils rather than chiefs, and there has always been a strong insistence on unanimous decisions, a custom which has slowed political movement and kept life relatively unchanged over the centuries.

In 1539 Estevan, a Moroccan Negro with an advance party of Coronado's troops and Mexican Indians, arrived at the pueblos. He was killed by the Zuni, but Coronado arrived soon after with his main force, bringing horses, mules, pigs, sheep and goats to winter in the pueblos along the Rio Grande. It was with difficulty that the pueblos were eventually subdued; missionaries were invariably killed for interfering in the religious dances. By 1598 the Spaniards moved in with serious intentions of colonization. It was not until 1680 that Pope, from the Tewa Pueblo, was able to raise a successful rebellion; the problem of unanimous tribal consent had posed endless difficulties. Finally, however, all but Isleta and Piro, remote Rio Grande villages, joined together and the Spanish were driven out. The Indians laid siege successfully to Santa Fe and the remaining Spanish fled. Pope ordered everything of Spanish origin destroyed, and the Indians agreed to this with the exception of fruit and vegetable seeds, which they regarded as sacred. The Pueblos then reasserted their own rule for twelve years, at which time the Spanish returned and conquered all but the peaceful Hopi, whom they seem to have overlooked. Despite their subjection to Spanish rule, the pueblo Indians kept on persistently with their religion and religious dances secretly within the kivas.

In recent times there has been controversy over the Sacred Blue Lake of Taos. Theodore Roosevelt created the Carson National Forest there, and the timber was to be protected until such time as needed by the lumber interests. However, pressure was brought to bear on the White House, and in turn on Congress, and in 1970 44,000 acres, including the Sacred Blue Lake, were restored to the people of Taos Pueblo.

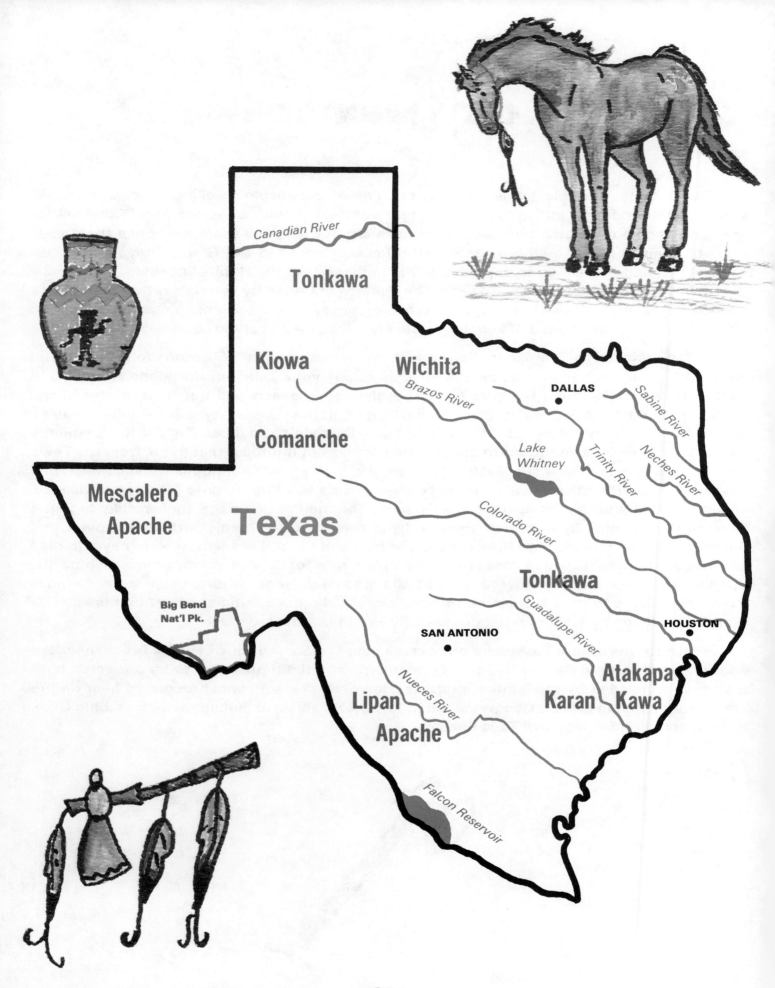

Canadian River

Tonkawa

Kiowa

Wichita

Brazos River

DALLAS

Sabine River

Neches River

Trinity River

Comanche

Lake Whitney

Mescalero Apache

Colorado River

Texas

Big Bend Nat'l Pk.

Tonkawa

Guadalupe River

HOUSTON

SAN ANTONIO

Nueces River

Atakapa Kawa

Karan

Lipan Apache

Falcon Reservoir

TEXAS

The geographical contrasts of Texas are very great; desert, plains, mountains, woodlands, and sub-tropical seacoast are all gathered into one political boundary. Indians have lived in these varied climates for many thousands of years, as shown by prehistoric pictographs and petroglyphs at Shumba Caves and Ballinger. Part of the Caddo group, the Nachitoches, and the Natsoo settled in Texas. The Mescalero Apaches, adamant and clever, roved the west central area, and just to the north of them were the Comanches, a Shoshonian group who had left their mountain homes with the advent of the horse. The Kiowa-Apaches, intelligent, fearless, and ready to fight, were in the northwest corner by the 1700s. Their two most famous leaders were Satanta and Setangya. The Tonkawas were a fierce plains people who were defeated and became scouts for the Texans against other Indian tribes. The Lipan Apaches in the west maintained a running fight against the Comanches as well as against the whites. They were a politically-minded people who tolerated missionaries.

The original natives called themselves "Tejas", or "Friendly People". Certainly their white visitors were not. Texas was a notorious haven for criminals, who had not come west to behave more responsibly toward Indians than they had toward their own countrymen. When Texas became a nation, Sam Houston tried unsuccessfully to protect the tribes, particularly the Cherokee, whose leader, The Bowl, was a close friend. The Comanche leaders, among them the half-white Quanah Parker, tried to achieve a series of peace treaties with the Texans, but to no avail.

Years later the official attitude of Texans, and of the government, was verbalized into history by General Philip Sheridan. On the banks of the Washita, where Custer had recently destroyed Black Kettle's village, Tochaway, a Comanche chief, announced solemnly and probably quite truthfully that Black Kettle was a good Indian. General Sheridan stated with heart-felt sincerity that the only good Indians he had ever seen were dead ones.

Papago

Lower California

Pima

Suma

Rio Grande

Rio

Yaqui

Concho

Yaqui

Mexico

Gulf
of
Mexico

Zacatec

Aztec

Rio Santiago

MEXICO CITY

Maya

YUCATAN
PENINSULA

Mixtec

Totonac

Oaxaca

Maya

Zapotec

Central
America

Miskito

Sumo

Ramah

CENTRAL AMERICA AND MEXICO

Like Canada and Alaska, these countries deserve a complete study of their own. Limited information is included here to make this overview of N. America complete.

These lands nearest to the equator supported some of the most sophisticated civilizations the world has ever known. Certain skills, customs, and religious beliefs filtered northward and are noticed among American tribes, especially in the Southeast.

It is believed that nomadic bands arrived in the Valley of Mexico some 12,000 years ago. The Olmec are considered to have set the earliest foundations of civilization there, and ruins of their architecture, as well as giant stone heads, are found in Tabasco and Vera Cruz. These people gained an understanding of mathematics and astronomy. Their influence extended south to the Maya, southwest to the Zapotec, and to the Totonac on their north. As a result, the Zapotecs had begun to develop politically and artistically, as did the Mixtecs to their north.

The beginnings of Mayan civilization remain a mystery, but we do know it lasted from 250-900 A.D. and then suddenly collapsed. During this period they developed a complex system of writing, and a knowledge of mathematics which included the concept of zero. They used their mathematical ability to move into astronomy, from which they invented their remarkable calendar, and their own version of astrology. The Mayans were a religious people. However, they surrendered much political power to their priests, who were the guardians of all knowledge. Their religious rites were based on human sacrifice, which demanded an ever-increasing supply of victims. The great Mayan ruins were Chichen Itza, Tullum, Uxmal, and Palenque in Yucatan; Copan in Honduras; and Tikal, Yaxchilan, and Uaxactun in Guatemala.

In the Ninth Century the Toltecs arrived, to become the greatest builders in Mexico. Art and artifacts reached new heights, and politics evolved in form and complexity. Illustrated documents were made on fine paper, elaborately processed. The invading Spaniards found Montezuma's capital to be a citadel of wealth and art as well as of highly developed knowledge. Only the wealth was appreciated by the invaders, and the great architecture was destroyed.

At its height, the Aztec Empire extended from the Gulf of Mexico to the Pacific Ocean. Corn was so easily grown that farmers had a surplus and so became traders as well. As with all Indians, land was not privately owned. The Aztecs are thought to have come to Mexico in the 1200s, and in 300 years they created a nation of tribute-paying cities, superb art, high politics, and an intelligent view of ecology, all to be delivered into the hands of the invading Spaniards.

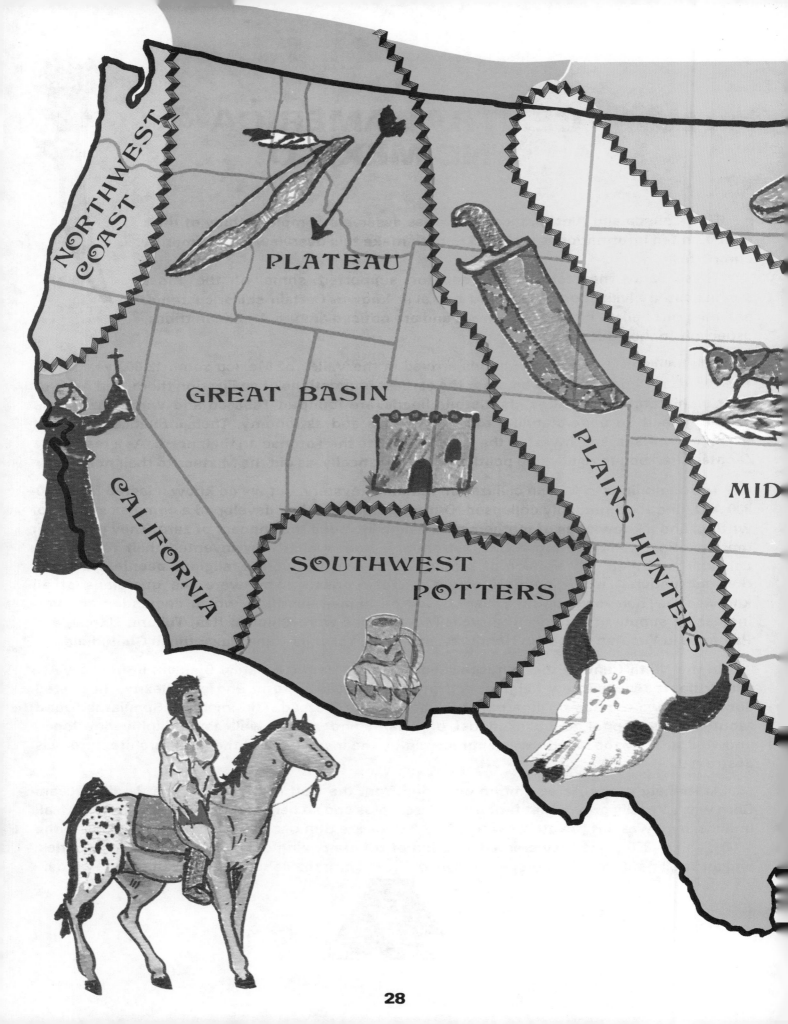

NORTHWEST COAST

PLATEAU

GREAT BASIN

CALIFORNIA

SOUTHWEST POTTERS

PLAINS HUNTERS

MID

NORTH WOODS
HUNTERS

NORTHEAST
WOODLAND

ST FARMERS

SOUTHEAST
FARMERS

MISSOURI, KANSAS AND NEBRASKA

A wide variety of tribes lived in this area, including the Osage, Kansa (or Kaw), Kiowa, Omaha, Pawnee, Wichita and Missouri. There were even Sioux in Nebraska. In the mid-nineteenth century, when the Indian world was in great flux, these and other tribes crisscrossed the region. Some of them live elsewhere today, but they are identified with this area insofar as they can be identified with any.

These Indian cultures produced many well-known Indians. For example, Maria Tallchief, the dancer, is an Osage. Acknowledged as one of the greatest ballerinas of all time (and the only American dancer ever to become a prima ballerina), she became famous throughout the world.

Charles Curtis, a Kansa (or Kaw), was the only Indian ever to serve as Vice President of the United States. He was in office from 1929 until 1933, under Herbert Hoover. He was a direct descendant of the Kansa chief, White Plume, and also of Pawhuska, an Osage chief. Starting life as a successful jockey, he later studied law, became a noted trial lawyer and was elected to Congress in 1892. He served fourteen years in the House and twenty in the Senate, where he was Republican whip. He was the author of the Curtis Bill for the protection of the Indians of the Indian Territory, and was responsible for much other legislation favorable to Indians, including a 1924 citizenship bill.

Dr. Susan La Flesche, an Omaha, was the first Indian woman to become a physician. Her father, Joseph, was the last recognized chief of the Omaha. She received her medical degree from the Women's Medical College of Philadelphia, and was then appointed physician for the Omaha Reservation. She cared for 1300 Indians under the most primitive conditions, traveling by horseback day and night, in all weather, without the help of any other physician and with no hospital. Her three sisters and single brother were hardly less remarkable. Her older sister, Susette, was the first Indian woman to speak for Indians internationally as well as nationally; and her brother, Francis, became a famous anthropologist.

Cheyenne
Omaha

Nebraska

Pawnee
Oto

Arapaho
Omaha

Osage
TOPEKA
Kansa
•

Kiowa
Kansas
Oto

Arkansas River
Kaw
Osage

Wichita

Mississippi River

Missouri River

Missouri

Missouri

MINNESOTA AND IOWA

There were several tribes in Minnesota usually associated with the West or Canada: the Arapaho, Cheyenne, Assiniboine, Chippewa (Ojibway), and Sioux (Lakota or Dakota). In fact, one of the bloodiest chapters in Sioux history took place in Minnesota, the famous Massacre of 1862. In 1851 the Minnesota Sioux (the four Dakota subtribes known as the Santee) had signed away their lands and gone on a reservation. The terms of the treaty were violated and they felt increasingly foolish and cheated. Finally the explosion came: under the leadership of Little Crow, they rose and killed some 700 settlers; a few women were also captured and subjected to the usual fate. The U.S. Army moved against them and suffered 100 dead, but put down the rebellion. Thirty-eight leaders were hanged at Mankato. Shortly afterward, a small Dakota war party murdered some settlers, and were quickly caught and executed on the spot. The Dakota started to flee Minnesota in earnest then, closely pursued by the Army. By 1865, this relentless harassment had forced the Dakota to the Missouri River and Minnesota was peaceful.

Minnesota is also the home of the Pipestone Quarry, the source of the beautiful red stone from which the ceremonial pipes were made. The quarry is said to have been the most important single place in the Indian world. The Sioux controlled it, and traded the pipes with tribes all over North America. Ownership has returned to the Yankton Dakota, and only Indian people are allowed to make use of the quarry.

It is of some importance to know that the word Sioux came from a Chippewa epithet for these people, given in answer to a question from the early French traders. "They are Nadowessioux," the Chippewa replied, "snakes or enemies." The French thought this was a tribal name and shortened it to Sioux. It has stuck, but the people in question dislike it, naturally preferring their own name for themselves: Dakota, or Lakota, meaning friends or allies.

Keokuk, Iowa, was named after the Sauk chief who led his people into Iowa after the War of 1812 and the consequent settlement of Illinois. This was the start of the struggle with Black Hawk, also a Sauk chief, who refused to leave Illinois. Otherwise, Iowa was curiously calm in the nineteenth century, an oasis in the midst of strife.

Chippewa

Red Lake

Dakota

Chippewa

Minnesota

Sauk & Fox

Mississippi R.

Santee Sioux

Minnesota R.

ST. PAUL

Pipestone Nat'l Mon.

Wahpeton

Yankton Sioux

Winnebago

Sauk & Fox

Des Moines R.

SIOUX CITY

Omaha

Iowa

CEDAR RAPIDS

COUNCIL BLUFFS

DES MOINES

Iowa

OKLAHOMA

In this state is found what may properly be called the remnants of the early Indian struggle. Behind it lay the defeats of the Iroquois, the Five Civilized Tribes (Cherokee, Choctaw, Creek, Seminole, Chickasaw), and all the other tribes east of the Mississippi. To the north were the disasters of the Plains Indians, to the Southwest the downfall of the Apache and Navajo, and to the west the final knell along the Pacific.

In all fairness, we should also know that Indians from the transplanted Oklahoma tribes have, as a state group, been more prominent and influential in state and national affairs than those of any other state.

Only the Osage have a reservation in Oklahoma; all other tribes there purchased or were given their own land. When the Five Civilized Tribes arrived in what was then the Indian Territory in the mid-nineteenth century, they bought all of what is now Oklahoma except the Panhandle. Each of those tribes established its own capitol, the Cherokee at Tahlequah, the Choctaw at Tahlihina, the Chickasaw at Tishomingo, the Creek at Okmulgee, and the Seminole at Wewoka. They re-established their own governments, including executive, legislative and judicial divisions, and each nation was treated as a separate political entity by the United States government. Churches, schools and towns were founded, and farms were built up.

It all came to naught because they sided with the Confederacy in the Civil War, and their lands were later confiscated. (Some of the confiscated land was given to newly arrived tribes as they were driven in from the east.) A small portion of the land was returned, after the white settlers had taken what they wanted. It would be a mistake to believe that the Civilized Tribes could have held onto their lands if they had not sided with the South; the idea that a handful of Indians would have been able to retain ownership of the entire state of Oklahoma is unthinkable.

Other tribes shipped into Oklahoma over the years include the Biloxi, Caddo, Delaware, Fox, Illinois, Iowa, Kickapoo, Miami, Missouri, Muskogee, Natchez, Ottawa, Peoria, Ponca, Sauk, Seneca, Shawnee, and Wyandot. All were driven from their original homes and all settled in Oklahoma on lands taken from the Five Civilized Tribes. These were not entire tribes, of course, but the tattered remains. Native to Oklahoma were small bands of Osage and Pawnee.

There is a graveyard at Fort Sill, Oklahoma, in which many of the great Plains leaders lie buried, especially Kiowa and Apache. Geronimo lies there, as do Setanka, Quanah Parker, Kicking Bird, and many others. It is known, fittingly enough, as the Indian Arlington.

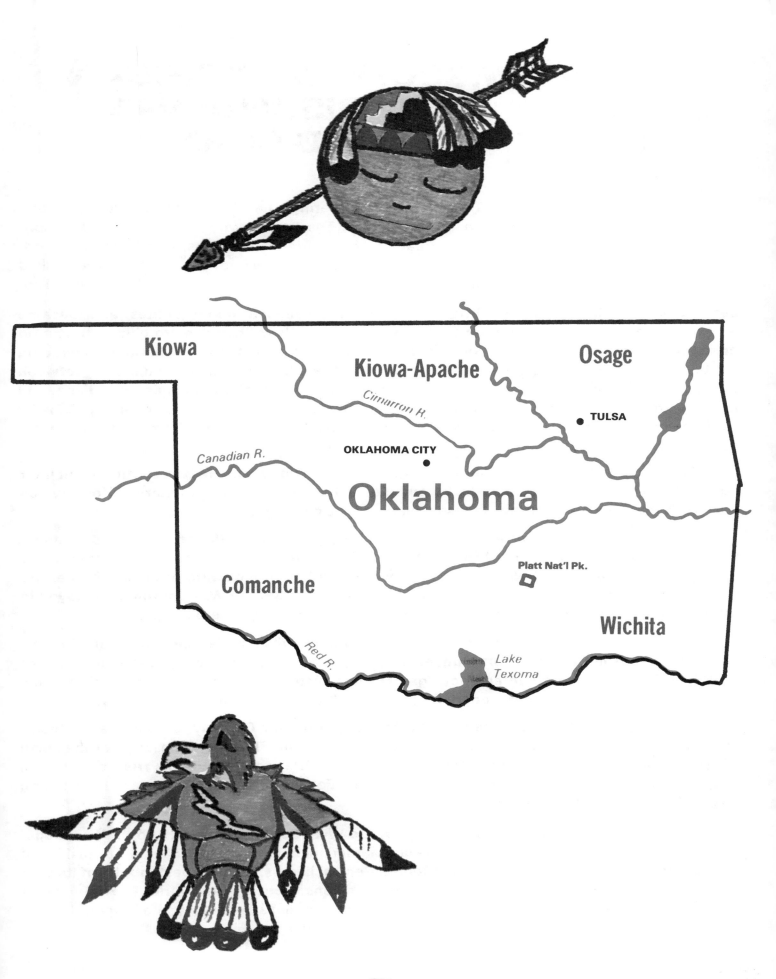

Kiowa

Kiowa-Apache

Osage

Cimarron R.

● TULSA

Canadian R.

OKLAHOMA CITY
●

Oklahoma

Comanche

Platt Nat'l Pk.

Wichita

Red R.

Lake
Texoma

WISCONSIN, MICHIGAN, ILLINOIS, INDIANA AND OHIO

These states, bordering the Great Lakes, are especially rich in Indian history. Tecumseh, whom many historians consider the greatest of all American Indians, was born near modern Springfield. His father and two of his brothers were killed in border skirmishes and fights such as the Battle of Fallen Timbers, against "Mad Anthony" Wayne. Although Tecumseh hated whites and became an extraordinary military leader, he also persuaded his fellow Shawnees to give up torturing prisoners, and he would not permit any woman or child to be harmed, including whites. He tried to form a confederacy to enforce the Ohio River as the boundary between the races, and failed when his brother precipitated the battle of Tippecanoe, in Indiana, and lost. In the War of 1812, Tecumseh sided with the British and was killed in Canada. American soldiers gave grisly evidence of his prominence by tearing off strips of his skin for souvenirs.

Black Hawk, a Sauk born in Illinois, fought the whites for years. He was captured, but later released and became a hero of sorts. When he died, he was buried in a military uniform which was a gift from General Andrew Jackson, along with a cane from Henry Clay.

Little Turtle, a Miami, was another Indian military genius. He inflicted crushing defeats on Generals Harmer and St. Clair in 1790 and 1791, the latter one of the worst defeats ever suffered by any American army, with 900 dead. He later gave up fighting, bowing to the inevitable, and was showered with official gifts. He was a close friend of George Washington, and stayed in his home for several weeks. On his death, he was given a military funeral.

Pontiac, an Ottawa, loved the French and hated the English. He led the French and Indians to victory over the British at Fort Duquesne. Later, after the English drove the French out of Fort Detroit, he formed a confederacy against them. After some successes, he had to make peace. He was later killed near modern St. Louis by a Kaskaskia Indian in English pay.

In addition to the tribes already cited, the Chippewa (or Ojibway, as they called themselves) ranged along the shores of Lakes Huron and Superior. They were the largest tribe north of Mexico, and because they were the first tribe in the area to get firearms from the French, they were able to drive the Sioux (Dakota), Sauk and Fox out and west. They are still the fourth largest tribe in the United States.

Also worthy of mention are the Kickapoo, the Wyandot (or western Huron), Winnebago, and Illinois (or Illiniwek) Confederacy. The last-named included the Cahokia and Kaskaskia. Of further interest is the fact that Cahokia Mound, Central Illinois, is the largest mound of its type north of Mexico, and the largest prehistoric earthen construction in the world. The mound was part of a city covering six square miles with a large residential area! Finally, the Serpent Mound in Ohio is the largest and finest serpent effigy in the country.

Lake Superior

Ojibway

Ottawa

Menomini

Mich

Ojibway

Ottawa

Lake Huron

Ojibway

Winnebago

Ottawa

Wisconsin

igan

Ojibway

Lake Michigan

Huron

Mississippi R.

MILWAUKEE •

Sauk & Fox

Potawatomi

CHICAGO •

DETROIT •

Kickapoo

Miami

Lake Erie

Illinois

Wyandot

Peoria

Illinois

Erie

SPRINGFIELD •

Indiana

COLUMBUS •

Cahokia Mound ▪

Wea

Ohio

• INDIANAPOLIS

ST. LOUIS •

Shawnee

Shawnee

Serpant Mound ▪

Cahokia

Kaskaskia

Yuchi

Ohio R.

37

KENTUCKY AND TENNESSEE

It is assumed from what evidence exists that the area of Kentucky was used as a general hunting park for many tribes. The name is from the Iroquois, Ken-Tapke, meaning "splendid fields." In the 1600s the Iroquois, with their newly-acquired guns, drove out the other tribes who had been sharing this primeval game preserve. Later a band of Shawnee formed a village in what is now Clark County. Lower Shawneetown was settled by small groups of Shawnee, Delaware, and Mingo. When these towns were abandoned in 1729, Indian residence in Kentucky was ended.

There are ancient ruins in the state of Tennessee which show that man has lived here many thousands of years. Near Manchester is Old Stone Fort, with walls twenty feet thick. The origins of this remarkable feat of engineering are unknown. In Madison and Cheatham Counties are large religious mounds. There are remains of cave and cliff dwellings and circular houses thirty feet in diameter. There are also mounds on Chickamauga Creek, and relics from the Yuchi, who lived by the Little Tennessee River. Near Memphis is the meticulously restored Chucalissa Prehistoric Indian Town.

The two major Indian tribes in the area were the Cherokee, a branch of the Iroquois, and the Chickasaw, who were related to the Muskhogean Nation. The Chickasaw were a small but powerful group. The Shawnee, a nomadic band of the Algonkian, arrived late and set up villages near what is now Nashville. The Cherokee and the Chickasaw, however, were able to drive them out.

A chief named Dragging Canoe, dissatisfied with a treaty, later broke away from the main Cherokee tribe and set up villages with his followers, becoming the Chickamauga. Outlaw whites joined them, and they raided the homes and towns of white settlers for many years.

After the Revolutionary War, the entire Cherokee Nation banded together to resist white usurpation of their lands, and the remaining Chickamauga rejoined them.

Kentucky

FRANKFORT

Mammoth Cave
Nat'l Pk.

MANCHESTER

Kentucky
Lake

Yuchi

NASHVILLE

Cherokee

Tennessee

Tennessee R.

Chickamauga

Great Smoky Mt.
Nat'l Pk.

Chickasaw

MEMPHIS

NORTH CAROLINA

The Indians of North Carolina began to settle in villages in prehistoric times. These were the peaceful Early Farmers, who were eventually driven out by more warlike tribes from the south. The fierce invaders built more permanent towns surrounded by stockades, with mounds for their temples. Town Creek Indian Mound has been authentically restored, and serves as an excellent example of this period.

There were probably 35,000 Indians in North Carolina at the time of the first European explorations into the area. In 1540 DeSoto came into the western mountains, seeking gold. Even earlier, in 1524, Verrazzano had searched the coast for the same purpose. The Indians Manteo and Wanchese were taken to England in 1584 by the Raleigh Company and made a profound and lasting impression. The important tribes in the 16th century were the Tuscarora, which numbered over 15,000, the Hatteras, Pamlico, Chowanoc, Cherokee and Catawba. An outdoor drama, The Lost Colony, near Manteo depicts the mystery of an early English colony's disappearance.

Today these tribes are all gone, except for a fragment of the Cherokee living in the west of the state, at the edge of the Great Smoky Mountain National Park. What little they have left of their once vast domain is home to these people, who are educated and live as modern Americans, but who also usually return "unto these hills" to retire no matter what their success in the white world.

The Cherokee were a peaceful, industrious hunting and farming people who tried to adapt to the white invasion. Despite the efforts of their remarkable leaders and the help of some whites, most of the Cherokees were deported in 1838 to the western Indian Territory along the Trail of Tears, where thousands perished. This portion of Cherokee history is depicted today in the outdoor drama, Unto These Hills, presented in Cherokee nightly during the summer. Those who are now in North Carolina are descendants of tribal members who hid in the deep coves and then fought to remain. The heroes of the Cherokee are Tsali, who gave his life to spare the fugitives; Sequoyah, who invented the Cherokee alphabet; Junaluska, who served under Andrew Jackson; and John Ross, an honorable political leader.

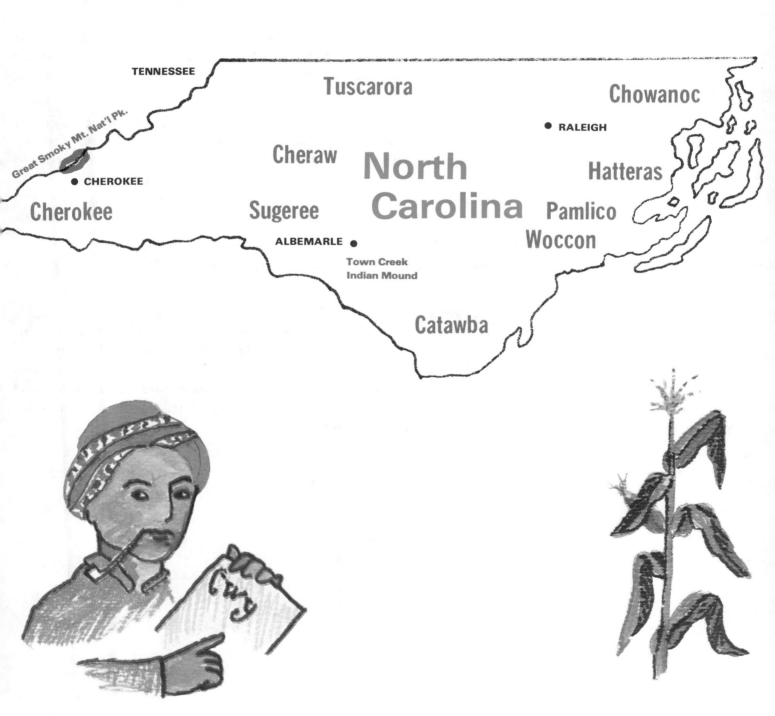

TENNESSEE

Tuscarora

Chowanoc

Great Smoky Mt. Nat'l Pk.

● RALEIGH

• CHEROKEE

Cheraw

North Carolina

Hatteras

Cherokee

Sugeree

Pamlico

Woccon

ALBEMARLE ●

Town Creek
Indian Mound

Catawba

FLORIDA

Florida was the early home of the Timucua, the Apalachee, and numerous smaller bands. The Spanish at one time experimented with a Christian Indian state; no colonists were allowed to settle, only the missionaries who were in charge of this noble attempt. The result was the destruction of these rather successful missions by invading Creek and Yuchi soldiers, working for English slavers, who carried off the inhabitants.

Eventually a branch of the notoriously militant Creeks pushed down into Florida and became known as the Seminoles, a word roughly translated as "those who broke away." These people adapted well to their new sub-tropical environment and were able to put up a powerful resistance when eventually attacked.

In the general removal of Indians from the Southeast, the Seminoles were overlooked for a while. Eventually it became their turn, and they were ready. They fell back into the swamps to wage all-out guerilla warfare. Their leader, the half-white Osceola, was captured treacherously under a flag of truce, and died in an inhuman military prison. Before he died, George Catlin painted an affecting portrait of him. Peace was finally achieved, but the Seminoles never surrendered. By the time that was over in 1842, it had cost the United States government $20,000,000 and the lives of nearly 2000 troops.

Today, some of the tribal members still live in the more remote part of Big Cypress, where they raise cattle on this inhospitable land.

The unique Seminole clothing, which they adapted from the English dress of a long-gone era, is bought by tourists from around the world. These shirts and dresses of patchwork and rickrack are considered well worth the high prices they bring. At the lower tip of the state live the Miccosukee in several small villages, with a school of their own amid the summer sleeping houses, called chickees. The Miccosukee have strong leadership, a well-planned educational program in a beautiful school, and a charming annual Art Festival which takes place in the winter months. They are a small but strong and contemporarily important tribe.

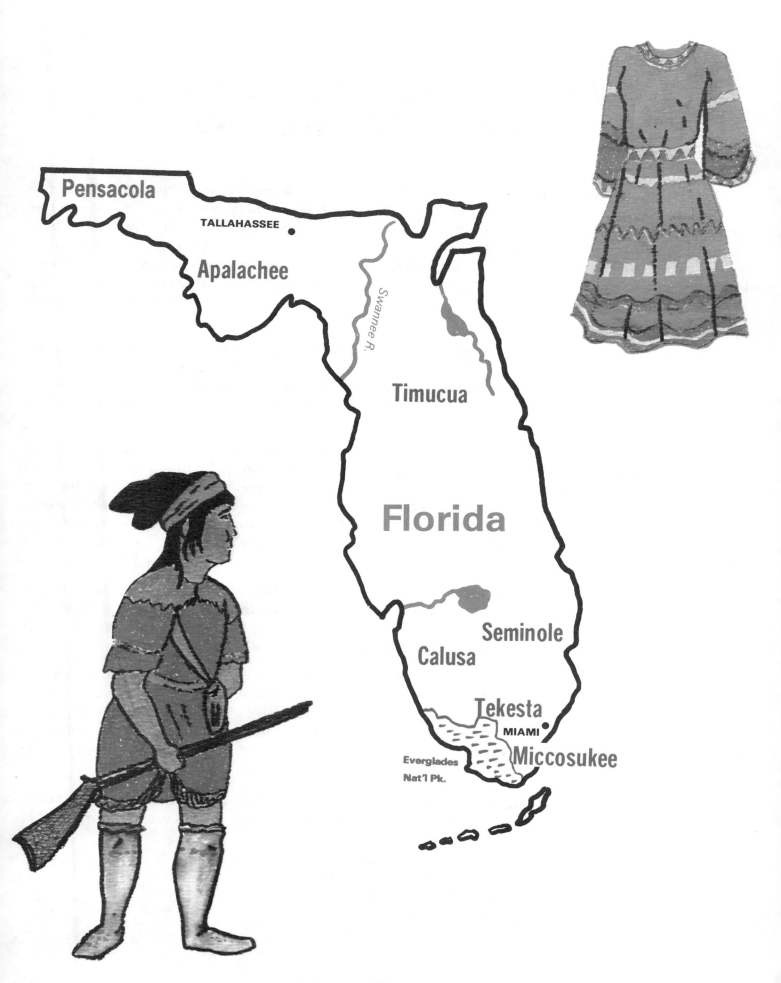

Pensacola

TALLAHASSEE •

Apalachee

Swannee R.

Timucua

Florida

Seminole

Calusa

Tekesta

MIAMI •

Miccosukee

Everglades
Nat'l Pk.

ALABAMA, GEORGIA AND SOUTH CAROLINA

We have considered the Cherokee in North Carolina, the Seminole in Florida, and the Choctaw in Mississippi, but there were members of those tribes in this area as well. Along with the Creek and Chickasaw, of whom we shall speak here, they comprised the Five Civilized Tribes, because they were either so highly advanced or becoming advanced, especially in the ways of white culture. Eventually the great majority of the Five Civilized Tribes were broken and driven into western exile, after they had made a valiant effort to adapt themselves to white ways. Indeed, they did adapt successfully; had it not been for the telltale skin color they would have been completely accepted.

The Creek, so named because their cultivated land stretched along the creeks of Georgia and Alabama, were typical of the others. They lived in the almost unbroken forest which once extended from the Mississippi to the Atlantic, laced with rivers and offering food of every kind: nuts, berries, fish, fowl and game. With such abundance they did not need to practice agriculture as they did.

The southeastern tribes enjoyed war, and were not averse to allying themselves with one white group against another. For example, the Creek joined the South Carolina British in 1680 in destroying the Christianized Spanish Indians in Georgia. Because the British offered the best trade goods bargains, the Creek remained their allies, and gradually bartered away their lands. After the British were ousted in the Revolutionary War, the Creek realized, too late, that they were at the mercy of the Americans. They started to resist and were put down brutally by Andrew Jackson in 1814.

Once they understood that peace and cooperation were their only hope, the Creek followed the Cherokee lead and compiled written codes of laws in English, and became literate in their own language. Hymns and translations of the Bible appeared; and mixed-blood leaders wrote letters in English and journeyed north to protect their rights. All to no avail.

From 1780 on, some Creek had seen the handwriting on the wall and had begun migrating west. The main body of the Creek were driven out in 1836-1840, selling their cattle and improvements at great loss. It is interesting that many of the Creek chiefs who advised the move were bribed to do so. Of the $247,000 paid to the Creek to move, $160,000 went to individual chiefs. They had learned what money meant in the modern world, and from then on the tribes were never free of graft.

In the section on OKLAHOMA, we see how they created a new life there. Nothing could ever replace the lost lands, though, nor compensate for the killing march west, epitomized in this Creek song, composed by a broken-hearted woman:

> I have no more land
> I am driven away from home
> Driven up the red waters
> Let us all go
> Let us all die together

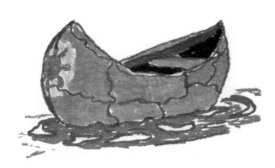

Yuchi

Tuskegee

Cherokee

Catawba

Pee Dee

COLUMBIA

Saluda R.

Pee Dee R.

Creek

South
Carolina

Santee

Coosa

ATLANTA

Clark
Hill
Res.

Alabama

Coosa R.

Creek

Alabama

Okmulgee

Savannah R.

Creek

Coosa

CHARLESTON

Georgia

Alabama R.

Seminole

Flint R.

Yamasee

Quale

Chactot

Mobile

Lake
Seminole

Okefenokee Swamp

MOBILE

45

MISSISSIPPI, LOUISIANA, ARKANSAS

Many of the original tribes in this area were mound builders. Indeed, the plazas and pyramids at Coles Creek, Louisiana, and the Emerald Mound, in Mississippi, show definite similarities to Mayan temples, giving rise to the theory that these peoples may have had a close connection with Mexico or Central America. Mounds were still being built as recently as the sixteenth century, when DeSoto came through.

The possibility of a connection is strengthened by the customs of the Natchez, who lived near the Emerald Mound. Their system was so unlike the usually democratic American Indian cultures that it has been the subject of exhaustive investigation, and remains a fascinating mystery.

The seven Natchez villages were ruled by an absolute monarch, known as the Great Sun. No one was permitted to address him except from a distance and with knees to the ground. He was carried in a litter so that his feet did not come in contact with the earth. He was at the top of a social system which rested on definite classes, progressing downward from Suns through Nobles and Honored Men to the common people, whom the French called Puants, or Stinkards.

The Natchez worshipped in an elevated temple with a perpetual fire and a god-image, tended by special priests. The Suns could only marry Stinkards, and if a Sun displeased his wife she could have him killed by snapping her fingers. He also had to stand in her presence, and could never sit with her. The Natchez flattened their foreheads back to a point, by binding, and had peculiar hair styles. One side of the head might be shaved, for instance, with long locks on the other. They were tattooed from head to foot, and the men carried fans. A far cry from the Iroquois or Sioux!

The Natchez were exploited by the French, arriving up the Mississippi, and finally fought back. They were defeated, and the Great Sun and many of his followers were sold into slavery in Santo Domingo. Others were burned in a public display. The few remaining joined other southeastern tribes, where they were considered mystics because of their ancient, sun-based religion.

Other famous tribes in this area were the Choctaw, Chickasaw and Yazoo in Mississippi, and the Caddo Confederacy in Arkansas and Louisiana.

Bull Shoals Lake

White R.

Arkansas R.

Chickasaw

• LITTLE ROCK

Arkansas

Caddo

Quapaw

Choctaw

Ouachita R.

Yazoo

Mississippi

Nachitoches

Caddo

Natchez

Mississippi R.

Natchez

• JACKSON

Pearl R.

Red R.

Pascagoula

Biloxi

Nachitoches

BATON
• ROUGE

Louisiana

Washa

• NEW ORLEANS

Lake Charles

VIRGINIA AND WEST VIRGINIA

When the white settlers arrived in Jamestown, there were three Indian confederations in Virginia: the Manahoac, the Monacan, and the Powhatan. The first two were comparatively small; the Powhatan was tremendous, composed of over thirty tribes and two hundred villages, each ruled by a minor chief. The chief of the entire Confederacy was Wahonsonacock. The English found this name too difficult, and called him Powhatan after the Confederacy itself. He was about sixty at the time, and it seems that he had painstakingly put the entire Confederation together in his own lifetime.

We are familiar with the story of his daughter, Pocahontas. Again, there was the inevitable language confusion. Her real name was Matowaka; Pocahontas was a nickname meaning "Frisky." She not only saved John Smith's life, but the very existence of the colony. The settlers said she, " . . . next to God, was the instrument to preserve the colony from death, famine and utter confusion," a sentiment inscribed on the statue to her at Jamestown.

Relations between the Indians and the colonists veered between peaceful and warlike. "Why should you take by force from us that which you can obtain by love? Why should you destroy us who have provided you with food?" These were the unanswerable questions put by Powhatan to Captain Smith. The Indians often brought food to the starving colonists; when the roles were reversed, the English governor gave 400 bushels of corn to some starving Indian villages only in return for "a mortgage on their whole countries," according to Smith.

Tobacco wore the land out, and new fields had to be found every two or three years. The colonists' appetite for land was never satisfied. Old Powhatan died in 1618 and was succeeded by his brother Opechancanough, an English-hater. In the spring of 1622 he loosed his warriors in a savage attack that took the lives of nearly 350 colonists in a few hours. Five years before this would have wiped out the colony, but it had quadrupled in those five years, and the surviving English swore to exterminate the Powhatans. It took about twenty years to do it, and the Indians made some devastating counterattacks, but it was finally done. Less than forty years after the founding of Jamestown, the once mighty Powhatan were penned up in a few small reservations and reduced to beggary. A hundred years or so later, at the time of the American Revolution, they were reduced to less than a thousand persons. Today, three of the Powhatan tribes still exist in Virginia; the Chickahominy (the largest numerically, they do not live on a reservation as do the other two); the Pamunkey; and the Mattaponi.

"All of these tribes made use of the territory that included much of West Virginia"

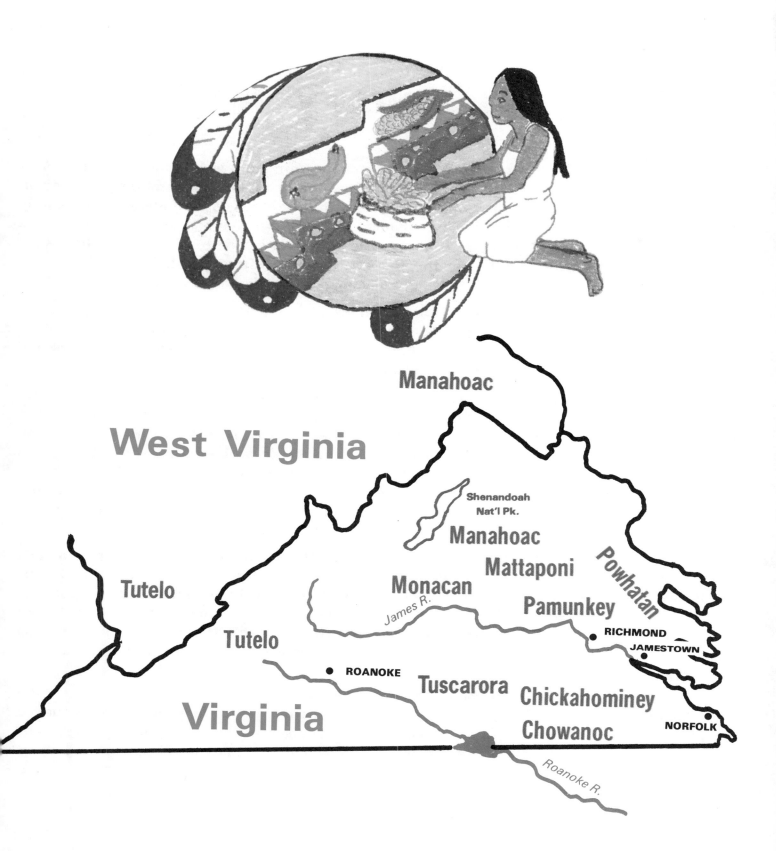

Manahoac

West Virginia

Shenandoah
Nat'l Pk.

Manahoac

Mattaponi

Tutelo

Monacan

James R.

Pamunkey

Powhatan

RICHMOND

JAMESTOWN

Tutelo

ROANOKE

Tuscarora

Chickahominey

Virginia

Chowanoc

NORFOLK

Roanoke R.

NEW YORK

Modern New York, stretching from Long Island on the Atlantic Seaboard to Lake Erie in the west, once contained several different Indian cultures. On Long Island were the Montauk, a confederacy containing, among others, the Shinnecock and the Manhasset. Also there were such individual tribes as the Rockaway and the Canarsee. They were later overrun by the Pequot and the Narragansett. Except for a few mixed-bloods, they have all joined other tribes or disappeared.

To the west were the Wappinger, a confederacy on the Lower Hudson River, and the Manhattan, a small tribe, which achieved immortality by selling an island for twenty-four dollars. It might be noted that the Manhattan also had fertile New Jersey meadows and probably didn't consider a rocky little island as worth any more than that.

However, it is the legendary Iroquois confederacy known as the Five Nations, Seneca, Cayuga, Onondaga, Oneida, and Mohawk, that controlled the great part of New York. The Iroquois moved through several distinct stages in their history. At first, as immigrants, they barely held their own against the Algonkians. Essentially an agricultural people, they were village dwellers living in longhouses, and organized into an elaborate matriarchal clan society. The clans, in turn, sent a total of fifty delegates to the confederacy, which had been organized for mutual protection. Although a relatively peaceful people, the early Iroquois tortured and ate captives.

With the advent of the white man, the Iroquois became trappers, and then a ferocious military power. When their own supply of beaver ran out, they attacked their neighbors, especially the Huron, looting furs or forcing acceptance as middlemen. They wiped out Huronia, the Neutral Nation, the Erie Nation, and the Susquehannock, all by 1653. It was of great importance to the English that the Iroquois were allied with them rather than with the French. If it had been the other way, North America might have become French rather than English.

The Iroquois were thus on the winning side in the French and Indian War, but in the American Revolution Joseph Brant went against a League vote for neutrality and persuaded most of the Nations to side with the British. The American victory destroyed the League and dispersed the Nations into Canada and the West. Those who remained in New York live on six reservations. One faction still considers itself a separate nation, senior to the United States, whose citizenship they reject.

Algonkian

Lake Champlain

Vermont

St. Lawrence Seaway

Adirondaks

Iroquois

Seneca

Mohawk   Mohican

Oneida

Lake Ontario

New York   • ALBANY

Cayuga

Niagara Falls

Onondaga

Lake Erie

Finger Lakes

• JAMESTOWN

Hudson R.

Wappinger
Man-
hatten

Shinnecock
Montauk
Manhasset

LONG ISLAND

PENNSYLVANIA, NEW JERSEY, DELAWARE AND MARYLAND

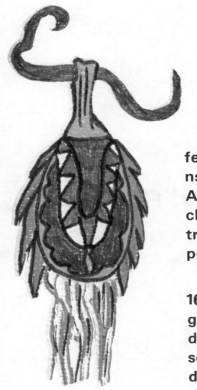

The Delaware, the most important of the eastern Algonkian confederacies, occupied most of New Jersey, Delaware and eastern Pennsylvania. They were called "grandfathers" by several other eastern Algonkian, especially the Nanticoke, Shawnee, and Mahican, who claimed descent from them. The confederacy included a number of subtribes, among them the Munsee, who were also considered a separate people.

William Penn concluded his famous treaty with the Delaware in 1682, and for a time they lived in peace with the whites. But they were gradually crowded out, with the approval of the Iroquois, under whose domination they had fallen around 1720, as the latter pressed south in search of fur pelts. They eventually crossed into Ohio, beginning an endless series of moves which ended with most of them incorporated with the Cherokee in Oklahoma. Others joined the Caddo and Wichita. The Moravian Christian Delaware were routinely massacred by frontiersmen in 1782.

This peaceful, civilized confederation stands symbolic of the many lesser-known Indian cultures which were wiped out. The Delaware chiefs, or sagamores, inherited through the male line. They ruled generally through persuasion rather than force. The medicine man, or shaman, had considerable influence. Life flowed between primitive agriculture, hunting, and rather random warfare.

There was considerable preoccupation with the spirit world, to which offerings of tobacco were given. The Great Being was also the Owner, and a sort of savior, named Gluskabe, devoted his time to setting right what the Great Being had failed to perfect in the original creation.

Wampum was not merely shell money, but possessed a sacred significance. It was called the "white string," "the old dark string," or "Indian stones." In the Algonkian language, in which there are different plural forms for animate and inanimate nouns, wampum was always animate.

In the soft, slow Delaware world, life was rather dreamlike, with no sharp demarcation between the real and the spiritual. Unconcerned with political and military ambitions, compared to the Iroquois for example, they drifted along, slowly and inevitably, to their destiny at the hands of the whites.

Erie

Munsee

Delaware

Allegheny R.

Pennsylvania

Delaware R.

New Jersey

Delaware

HARRISBURG

PHILADELPHIA

TRENTON

Susquehanna

Delaware

Potomac R.

Maryland

BALTIMORE

Nanti-
coke

DOVER

Delaware

MAINE, NEW HAMPSHIRE, VERMONT, MASSACHUSETTS, CONNECTICUT AND RHODE ISLAND

This was the home of those Indians who met the Pilgrim Fathers and taught them to plant corn and fertilize with fishheads. They gave us such words as "squash," "succotash," "hominy," "moose," "squaw," "papoose," and "tomahawk." They were the Algonkian tribes, the Abnaki, Massachusett, Narraganset, Wampanoag, Pennacook, Pequot, and Mahican (known as the Mohegan in Connecticut). They survive mainly as mixed-bloods; as a people they have long disappeared, among the first to be exterminated.

These Algonkians lived in small villages of domed wigwams covered over with bark or skin. They raised corn, fertilizing the fields with fishheads; indeed, the cornfields were deliberately planted near the rivers where the fish known as alewives swarmed up in the spring. They hilled the corn to strengthen the roots and tended it carefully all summer.

The eastern Algonkian, unfortunately, lived directly in the path of the arriving colonists. In addition to the usual white desire for land, there was also the struggle between England and France, a struggle which was to end in the near extinction of Indian life along the Atlantic Coast. Their first contact with white men, long before the Puritans arrived, was with the hundreds of cod fishermen who camped along the Maine coast. Then came the settlers, and the inevitable chain of events: the friendliness of the initial meeting, the growing awareness of the irreconcilable differences in attitude about property and, finally, the open warfare.

We are familiar with the touching story of Pilgrim-Indian friendship. We may not know Captain John Underhill's description of his 1637 destruction of a stockaded Pequot town on the Mystic River: " . . . many courageous fellows . . . fought most desperately through the palisades so that they scorched and burned with the very flame . . . and so perished valiantly. Mercy did they deserve for their valor, could we have had opportunity to have bestowed it. Many were burned in the fort, both men, women and children. Others, forced out, came in troops . . . twenty and thirty at a time, which our soldiers received and entertained with the point of the sword . . ."

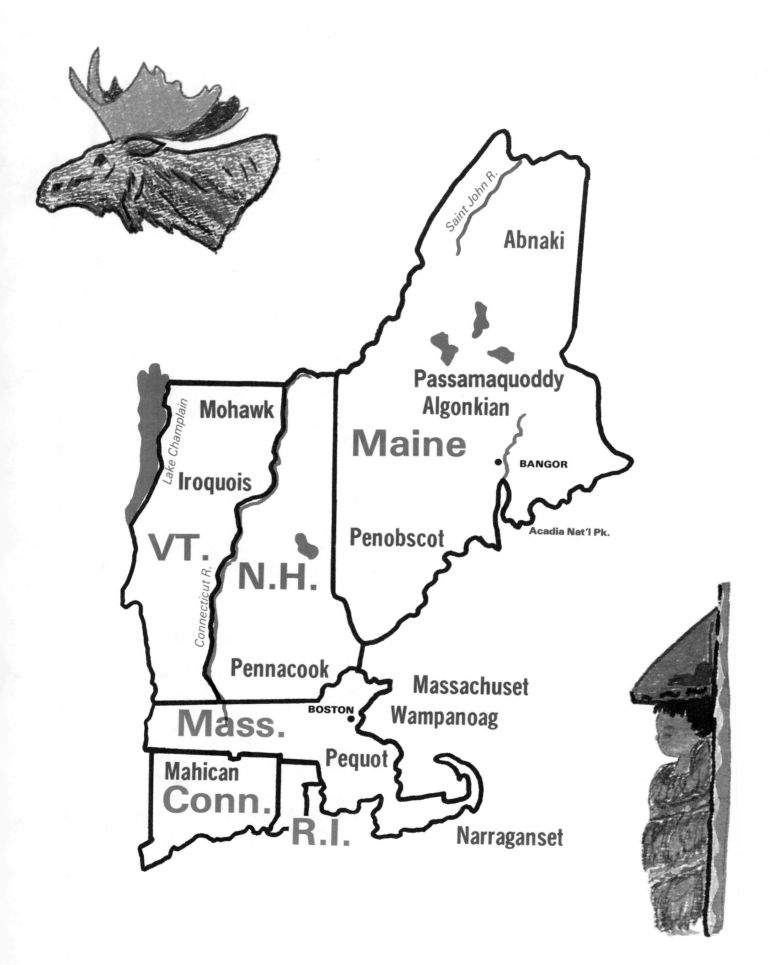

Saint John R.

Abnaki

Passamaquoddy
Algonkian

Mohawk

Lake Champlain

Iroquois

Maine

BANGOR

VT.

Connecticut R.

N.H.

Penobscot

Acadia Nat'l Pk.

Pennacook

Massachuset

BOSTON

Wampanoag

Mass.

Pequot

Mahican

Conn.

R.I.

Narraganset

55

SUGGESTED READING

The following books provide a firm general background on Indians in the Americas. They are all well written and make interesting reading.

Baldwin, Gordon C.	**Indians of the Southwest** G. P. Putnam
Blacker, Irwin R.	**Cortes and the Aztec Conquest** Harper and Row
Brandon, William	**American Heritage Book of Indians** Dell
Capps, Benjamin	**The Indians** Time-Life Books
Catlin, George	**(Many editions by various publishers)**
Collier, John	**Indians of the Americas** New American Library
Deloria, Vine	**God Is Red** Dell **We Talk, You Listen** Dell **Custer Died for Your Sins** Macmillan
Driver, Harold E.	**Indians of North America** University of Chicago Press
Eastman, Charles A.	**Indian Boyhood** Fawcett
Geronimo	**Geronimo, His Story** Dutton
Grinnell, George Bird	**The Cheyenne Indians** Cooper Square Publishers
Haines, Francis	**Indians of the Great Basin and Plateau** G. P. Putnam
Hassrick, Royal B.	**The Sioux** University of Oklahoma Press
Hyde, George E.	**Indians of the Woodlands** University of Oklahoma Press
Josephy, Alvin M., Jr.	**The Indian Heritage of America** Bantam
Kluckhohn, Clyde & Dorothea Leighton	**The Navajo** Doubleday
Neihardt, John G.	**Black Elk Speaks** Pocket Books
Neuberger, Richard Lewis	**The Lewis and Clark Expedition** Random House
Powers, William K.	**Indians of the North American Plains** G. P. Putnam **Indians of the Southern Plains** G. P. Putnam
Salomon, Julian Harris	**The Book of Indian Crafts and Lore** Harper and Row
Sandoz, Mari	**These were the Sioux** Dell
Wissler, Clark	**Indians of the United States** Doubleday